The
AMAZING
MACKEREL
PUDDING
PLAN

The AMAZING MACKEREL PUDDING PLAN

Classic Diet Recipe Cards from the 1970s

Wendy McClure

Riverhead Books,
New York

THE BERKLEY PUBLISHING GROUP
Published by the Penguin Group
Penguin Group (USA) Inc.
375 Hudson Street, New York, New York 10014, USA
Penguin Group (Canada), 90 Eglinton Avenue East, Suite 700, Toronto, Ontario M4P 2Y3, Canada
(a division of Pearson Penguin Canada Inc.)
Penguin Books Ltd., 80 Strand, London WC2R 0RL, England
Penguin Group Ireland, 25 St. Stephen's Green, Dublin 2, Ireland (a division of Penguin Books Ltd.)
Penguin Group (Australia), 250 Camberwell Road, Camberwell, Victoria 3124, Australia
(a division of Pearson Australia Group Pty. Ltd.)
Penguin Books India Pvt. Ltd., 11 Community Centre, Panchsheel Park, New Delhi—110 017, India
Penguin Group (NZ), cnr Airborne and Rosedale Roads, Albany, Auckland 1310, New Zealand
(a division of Pearson New Zealand Ltd.)
Penguin Books (South Africa) (Pty.) Ltd., 24 Sturdee Avenue, Rosebank, Johannesburg 2196, South Africa

Penguin Books Ltd., Registered Offices: 80 Strand, London WC2R 0RL, England

THE AMAZING MACKEREL PUDDING PLAN

While the author has made every effort to provide accurate telephone numbers and Internet addresses at the time of publication, neither the publisher nor the author assumes any responsibility for errors, or for changes that occur after publication. Further, the publisher does not have any control over and does not assume any responsibility for author or third-party websites or their content.

First Riverhead trade paperback edition: May 2006
Riverhead trade paperback ISBN: 1-59448-208-X

An application to register this book for cataloging has been submitted to the Library of Congress.

PRINTED IN MEXICO

10 9 8 7 6 5 4 3 2 1

For my mom
(who never makes these recipes),

and for Chris
(who might, if I dared him).

SOUPS, SALADS, SNACKS, SORROW

Did you know that some molded salads can blend into their surroundings to escape predators, just like chameleons? Observe the Spinach and Egg Mold as it begins to take on the appearance of the Formica countertop.

Then again, it didn't really have to worry about being eaten, anyway.

Budget Best Bets /20

SPINACH AND EGG MOLD

Weight Watchers® Recipe Cards

SURPRISE CHOWDER

Weight Watchers® Recipe Cards

Surprise chowder? Oh, goody, because nothing livens up a thick, translucent soup like a *sense of uncertainty!*

(I wonder if that dead, spiny plant is a hint.)

There's lettuce. There are pickles. There are capers. There's lime. There's parsley. There's celery inside. Chives, too. It's green. All green. No other guiding culinary principle except . . . GREEN.

It's a meal! It's an obsessive disorder! It's *both!*

Snacks, Beverages, and Light Meals /10

HOT WRAP UPS

Weight Watchers® Recipe Cards

ROSY PERFECTION SALAD

Weight Watchers® Recipe Cards

I don't think you're ready for this jelly.

I don't think you'll ever be. None of us will. No. No way.

Really, it's a shame more salads don't look like pimp hats.

Salads Hot and Cold /16

MADRILÈNE-CHEESE SALAD

Weight Watchers® Recipe Cards

PATRIOTIC SOUPS

Weight Watchers® Recipe Cards

Some freedom-hating soups want to take our spoons away and would have us slurp at the edge of our bowls like dirty foreigners. But these soups don't run!

You want them to taste good? What are you, a Communist?

Sometimes, all the photo stylist can do is use a prop so ugly it can only make the food look better in comparison. Thus, for the Pears That Look Like They've Gotten Sick on Them-selves, only the Sludge-Drooling Blowfish will do.

Convenience Fish /14

SALMON AND PEAR SALAD

Weight Watchers® Recipe Cards

MARCY'S "ENCHILADA"

Weight Watchers® Recipe Cards

We don't know who Marcy is, only that she thinks "enchilada" is wacky Mexican talk for "shit on a shingle."

Everyone thinks I should stop feeding my dogs because they're "not real." They think they're just "crappy knickknacks from the Dollar Store" that I bought before I "went off the medication."

But don't you think they look hungry? Here, Buster! Here, Dorothy Elvis Methuselah VI! Time for soup!

I'm sorry it's cold. I'm not allowed to use the stove anymore.

Snacks, Beverages, and Light Meals 5

COLD TOMATO SOUP

Weight Watchers® Recipe Cards

POLYNESIAN SNACK

Weight Watchers® Recipe Cards

Would you like Polynesian Snack? With beautiful flower?

Where is fork? Is Snack for to eat with hand?

You like canned bean sprout? And buttermilk? And pimiento? And fruit piece? Mix all together? No? Oh. Maybe Snack is not for you.

You know, I don't think I want to know why the cream is in quotes.

CUCUMBER "CREAM" SALAD

Weight Watchers® Recipe Cards

CHILLED CELERY LOG

Weight Watchers® Recipe Cards

You could eat this log. Or, you could stick your hand in a rusty kitchen grinder. Yeah, have fun.

Little is known about the People's Republic of Orienta, only that its people like Chinese knickknacks and canned food.

Convenience Fish /11

ORIENTAL TUNA SALAD

Weight Watchers® Recipe Cards

EGGPLANT CAVIAR

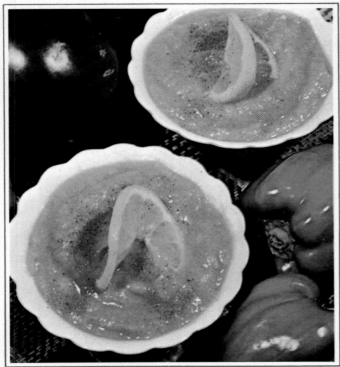

Weight Watchers® Recipe Cards

It only *tastes* like it came out of a fish's ass.

My guess is they tried being consistent with the plural at first, and then decided that "Snacks On Sticks" sounded too disturbing. Like *Apocalypse Now* food or something.

This is frozen coffee, people. It *almost* sounds kind of good, until you freeze a whole bunch and take them out and look at them and hit a few of them to-gether and hear them go *thunk, thunk,* and say, "Oh, fuck this shit," and drop the whole tray on the floor in disgust.

SNACKS ON A STICK

Weight Watchers® Recipe Cards

BEAN AND MUSHROOM SALAD

Weight Watchers® Recipe Cards

See how the ceramic mushroom family has gathered to show their children what happens to bad little mushrooms.

The Soup is Inspiration. The Soup is Love. Smell the Soup.

When one first arrives here, one may believe the Soup tastes like ass. That is not so, my child. The Soup is Inspiration and the Soup is Love. Your name is now "Harmonia." The Soup is Inspiration, and you do not want to leave. The Soup is Love, and we have an electrified fence. The Soup is Inspiration. And the Soup is Love.

Soups and Stews /**10**

INSPIRATION SOUP

Weight Watchers® Recipe Cards

MELON MOUSSE

Weight Watchers® Recipe Cards

"Ted and I were thinking—you know how we play doubles in tennis? And sometimes we, you know, *switch*? Well, it's 1974 and all, and . . . oh, yes, it's a little forward of us, but . . . well, why don't you two just try this *Melon Mousse* and think about it, okay?"

Soups, Salads, Snacks, Sorrow

19

When life gives you lemons, make a fucking mess.

How's *that* for piquant?

Convenience Fish /12

PIQUANT SALMON ON TOAST

Weight Watchers® Recipe Cards

FROZEN CHEESE SALAD

Weight Watchers® Recipe Cards

Well *of course* it's a salad; there are wooden salad utensils next to it, see? You take the spoon and whack at the block of frozen cheese . . . and . . . and . . . okay, nothing happens. Because it's *frozen cheese,* dumbass.

For when you're hungry after a long, busy day of playing rusty cowbells with a big wooden-knob thingy.

Or, you know, whatever.

Salads Hot and Cold

8

CURRIED CABBAGE AND EGG SALAD

Weight Watchers® Recipe Cards

MEXICAN SHRIMP-ORANGE SALAD

Weight Watchers® Recipe Cards

This is a salad best enjoyed at the home of the scary lady down the street who never leaves the house and talks to her knickknacks.

I showed this card to a friend who said, "What the hell's in that bowl? Bong water?"

That would at least explain why the ceramic animals are so drawn to it.

I never knew before now how much grated raw cauliflower looks just like shredded ceiling tile.

Asbestos: it's what's for lunch!

Salads Hot and Cold

4

CAULIFLOWER-ORANGE SALAD

Weight Watchers® Recipe Cards

Snacks, Beverages, and Light Meals /11

JELLIED TOMATO REFRESHER

Weight Watchers® Recipe Cards

Yes, let's have these in *brandy snifters.* Let's just tip our heads back and let the chunks slide in.

The time you spend eating these is time you'll want back at the very end of your life. That's why they're served with a clock.

Could this be Inspiration Soup in congealed gelatin form? Could it be that the Soup Cult has left its compound and moved to the suburbs? Where they serve beautifully arranged platters of *Molded Asparagus Salad* to innocent housewives? Who ingest the salad spiked with the mind-altering drugs that rob them of their free will? And give them hallucinations in which all the universe, save the Salad, is one vast, glowing, cyan void?

I mean, it's just a theory.

Salads Hot and Cold | 18

MOLDED ASPARAGUS SALAD

Weight Watchers® Recipe Cards

9

MOCK HERRING SALAD

Weight Watchers® Recipe Cards

Mock Herring Salad all you want but it'll never cry. *You*, on the other hand, have to eat this shit.

SAUCES,
LIGHT MEALS,
LUNCHES,
LOATHING

Once upon a time the world was young and the words *mackerel* and *pudding* existed far, far away from one another.

One day, that all changed. And then, whoever was responsible somehow thought the word *fluffy* would help.

Oh, and eggs, too.

Convenience Fish / 7

FLUFFY MACKEREL PUDDING

Weight Watchers® Recipe Cards

CRAB NEWBURG

Weight Watchers® Recipe Cards

Wow, Crab Newburg on pink velvet, and it's only your first date with the Miami drug lord.

He may have said it was white zinfandel in that glass, but I wouldn't drink it too fast if I were you.

I feel for the Hindu souls who were reincarnated as these shrimps. But then you have to wonder what they did in their past lives to deserve being re-born as the garnish for fake Indian food.

I mean, it must have been *really* bad.

Worldwide Favorites /21

STUFFED APPLES GANGES

Weight Watchers® Recipe Cards

/22

SPLIT PEA PATTIES

Weight Watchers® Recipe Cards

These patties are so seventies they have their own encounter group, man, where they sit in a circle talking about their feelings. And how do they feel? Like rancid ketchup and sawdust, mostly.

Oh, wait—that's how they *taste*.

It's provolone on tomato purée on white bread, which makes it neither "perfect" nor "pizza." And I bet you could lose the "lunch" part, too. Literally.

Snacks, Beverages, and Light Meals /14

PERFECT PIZZA LUNCH

Weight Watchers® Recipe Cards

HEARTY FISH CAKES

Weight Watchers® Recipe Cards

They're watching us. They're among us. They want us to think they're just seafood appetizers. "Hearty" ones, even—though of course they don't have hearts at all, just diabolical reptilian eyes. OH MY GOD, DID ONE JUST BLINK?

The Amazing Mackerel Pudding Plan

I hope that by "versatile" they mean "you can do something with this chicken besides *eat* it." Because clearly, each piece is its own self-contained Grow Your Own Deadly Bacteria kit. It's fun! It's easy! You don't even need a petri dish! It's just like having an ant farm.

Except, of course, with salmonella instead of ants.

Make-Ahead Main Dishes /22

VERSATILE CHICKEN IN ASPIC

Weight Watchers® Recipe Cards

36

ONION SAUCE

Weight Watchers® Recipe Cards

They call this "onion sauce," but it looks more like the end of a snuff film to me.

That's right—*fish* snuff. Die, fish, *die.*

Comes with its own commemorative plant and chicken effigy! After all, this lunch wouldn't even be possible without all the selfless chickens who put their names on the organ-donor registry.

Think of them, and *enjoy.*

CHOPPED CHICKEN LIVER

Weight Watchers® Recipe Cards

FISH "TACOS"

Weight Watchers® Recipe Cards

Mexican food is easy to make! All you need are toast and quotation marks! Just ask Marcy!

(I *so* do not understand the props here.)

Uh-oh. Marcy needs to be stopped.

NEW PIZZA SAUCE

Weight Watchers® Recipe Cards

The Amazing Mackerel Pudding Plan

FISH BALLS

Weight Watchers® Recipe Cards

My, they're much bigger than one would think.

The fisherman would like you to know that he has an impressive pair of buoys, too.

Cheese Bake Lunch! On plate serve thing! With coffee brew drink!

Make-Ahead Main Dishes / 3

CHEESE BAKE LUNCH

Weight Watchers® Recipe Cards

TUNA PUFF

Weight Watchers® Recipe Cards

"Tuna Puff" would be a great name for either a Sanrio character or a drag queen, but as you can tell, this dish is neither.

Chicken Liver Bake: enjoy it with the ashes of a loved one.

Or maybe the chickens *were* your loved ones, and what's left of them is what's in that urn.

Because chickens never love you back. And that's why you have to kill them. And eat their livers ritualistically. Then they're a part of you forever.

Forever.

Main Dishes in Minutes / 4

CHICKEN LIVER BAKE

Weight Watchers® Recipe Cards

MOUSSE OF SALMON

Weight Watchers® Recipe Cards

Sometimes salmon will come to the big city full of dreams, only to wind up used, and mangled, and reconstituted, and all tarted up in some kind of sick, horrifying salmon drag.

Look, it's still trying to spawn. With lemons. It's confused. Oh, man, so sad.

It's even more heartbreaking when they're young.

SHRIMP-SALMON MOLD

Weight Watchers® Recipe Cards

BROILED APPLEBURGERS

Weight Watchers® Recipe Cards

How American can apple pie be if it doesn't have *meat* in it? Enter the AppleBURGER, as beefy and wholesome as a small-town quarterback. Whose appetite is so hearty he needs to eat with a towel. Because napkins are for wimps. And buns are for flag-burners.

Simply replace the eggs on top with a little sign that says "Banana Bread," and *voila!* You'll never have to do another damn bake sale again.

Convenience Fish /16

SALMON CAKE

Weight Watchers® Recipe Cards

TUNA FISH CAVALIER

Weight Watchers® Recipe Cards

Cavalier on the outside. Crying on the inside.

These spicy meatballs are made with beef and lamb and topped with . . . melted yellow squirrel.

Because in 1974, it was okay to drop acid when your diet got a little dull.

Classic Adaptations   4

ĆEVAPĆIĆI (BEEF AND LAMB ROLLS)

Weight Watchers® Recipe Cards

Make-Ahead Main Dishes /14

MOLDED CHEESE SOUFFLÉ

Weight Watchers® Recipe Cards

Not only will the top of this soufflé never collapse, but it can also give you a therapeutic massage.

Sauces, Light Meals, Lunches, Loathing

Hint from Heloise #2137: If you want to make sure your dish isn't mistaken for a Christmas fruitcake, serve it with springlike daffodils.

The Amazing Mackerel Pudding Plan

Fish Spectaculars   /16

SALMON LOAF

Weight Watchers® Recipe Cards

BARBECUE SAUCE

Weight Watchers® Recipe Cards

Behold the only human presence in the whole series. Just that fleeting glimpse of life, the hand doing its job in its protective oven mitt, like a soldier in hazmat gear.

Wait. That mitt's only *pretending* to hold the saucepan. How do we know that sauce is really *pouring*? How do we know there's really a *hand* in that mitt? Or *chicken* on that platter? WHAT ELSE ARE THEY LYING TO US ABOUT?

MAKE-AHEAD MEAT CREATIONS, CASSEROLES, AND OTHER CREEPINESS

The first rule of Casserole Club is: You do not talk about Casserole Club.

The Amazing Mackerel Pudding Plan

CLUB DAY CASSEROLE

Weight Watchers® Recipe Cards

Make-Ahead Main Dishes /13

MEAT LOAVES WITH HORSERADISH

Weight Watchers® Recipe Cards

The wild kingdom of diet recipes is full of amazing true tales! These orphaned baby meat loaves were adopted by a pack of salad molds, who are now feeding them pimientos and lovingly raising them as their own.

Also known as "Scale Model of the Bayou."

PRIDE OF THE BAYOU

Weight Watchers® Recipe Cards

CABBAGE CASSEROLE CZARINA

Weight Watchers® Recipe Cards

This looks like hell but I sure dig the "Czarina" part. Would you enjoy Tuna Czarina, or Cottage Cheese Czarina, or Cream of Wheat Czarina? You almost would, right?

Okay, never mind.

Heh-heh, "beef loaf."

Oh, come on, you were thinking it, too.

Main Dishes in Minutes

2

BROILED BEEF LOAF

FRANKFURTER PIE

Weight Watchers® Recipe Cards

Frankfurters in a pie under a quilt.

You know how when you were a kid you walked in on your parents? And when you repressed the memory, it wound up looking like this? Good luck with therapy!

Make-Ahead Meat Creations, Casseroles, and Other Creepiness

The fact that the main selling point of this dish is, "You can make it using standard major appliances!" should tell you all you need to know.

Make-Ahead Main Dishes / 9

FREEZER-TO-OVEN VEAL DINNER

Weight Watchers® Recipe Cards

SWEET AND SOUR MEATBALLS

Weight Watchers® Recipe Cards

I don't want to eat these meatballs and cranberries so much as I want to string them on a festive garland. Meaty Christmas!

Evidently they misspelled "ghoulish."

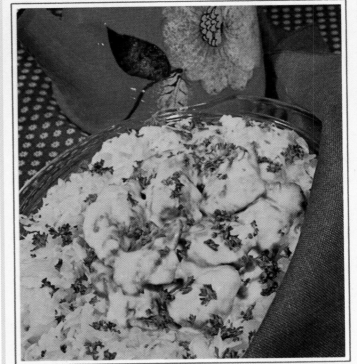

Worldwide Favorites /17

PORK GOULASH

Weight Watchers® Recipe Cards

CHOUCROUTE GARNIE

Weight Watchers® Recipe Cards

Oh, sure, maybe Julia Child thought she was all fancy when *she* made this dish, but did she think to make it with hot dogs? And garnish it with *acrylic plush*?

It took a genius to do that. And maybe drugs, too.

Well, as adjectives for *mackerel* go, *snappy* is better than *fluffy*. Snappy! So snappy you need *three* glasses of cranberry juice to wash it down! So snappy they've placed it in a special roped-off area! Don't get too close to the casserole! 'Cause it'll SNAP at ya! Ha! Ha! SNAPPY!

Convenience Fish /18

SNAPPY MACKEREL CASSEROLE

Weight Watchers® Recipe Cards

VEAL STEW

Weight Watchers® Recipe Cards

Grossing everyone the hell out is *one* way to win at dominoes, I guess.

Make-Ahead Meat Creations, Casseroles, and Other Creepiness

If you think this is bad, you should see what Morning-After Stew looks like.

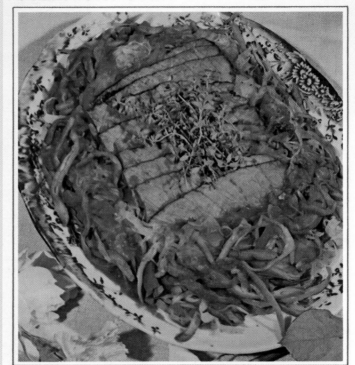

Make-Ahead Main Dishes /16

OVERNIGHT STEW

Weight Watchers® Recipe Cards

Fish Spectaculars

5

FISH JAMBALAYA

Weight Watchers® Recipe Cards

This dish is served . . .

a. on a bed of boiled celery instead of rice, dear God.
b. on "rice." Get it? "Rice"?
c. in an unfathomable parallel universe where Cajun food exists, but carbohydrates do not.
d. all of the above.

Make-Ahead Meat Creations, Casseroles, and Other Creepiness

69

Back in 'Nam, we had to be careful with our tuna casseroles. The VC could spot the ones made with noodles from fifty yards away, man. And those french-fried onions meant you were just *asking to be killed.*

No, the only way you could survive those potlucks was to master the art of casserole camouflage.

Convenience Fish /22

TUNA FISH CASSEROLE

Weight Watchers® Recipe Cards

MACKERELLY

Weight Watchers® Recipe Cards

Sometimes mere adjectives for *mackerel* are not enough. Sometimes *mackerel* is *mackerel* unto itself. Sometimes you just have to let go. Mackerelease yourself. Embrace mackereality.

Hey, kids! Math concepts come alive with the magic of ground veal! Can you calculate "two to the power of three" using these veal loaves? Let's find out!

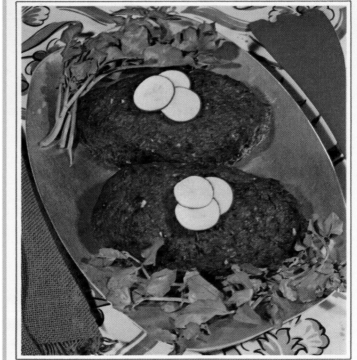

VEAL LOAVES WITH MUSHROOMS

Weight Watchers® Recipe Cards

VEAL-SAUERKRAUT CASSEROLE

Weight Watchers® Recipe Cards

Wow! That sure is a lot of veal! Who wants to count them and see what the answer is?

Anyone?

The Amazing Mackerel Pudding Plan

74

Um, Heidi? I have some bad news. It's about your goats.

SWISS STEW

Convenience Fish /23

TUNA HOT POT

Weight Watchers® Recipe Cards

Average score on IsMyHot-
PotHotOrNot.com: 2.

I know, Satan's a shitty cook, but *you* try telling him he can't come to the potluck.

You have to admit it's cool how the lid floats up all by itself, just like that kid in *The Exorcist*.

Fish Spectaculars / 3

DEVILED CRAB CASSEROLE

Weight Watchers® Recipe Cards

SLOPPY JOES MANILA

Weight Watchers® Recipe Cards

Take one ethnic cuisine, add gross misinterpretation. Stir well. Serve on toast.

Marcy has struck again.

MAIN DISH
MALEVOLENCE

When Sid and Marty Krofft originally created the puppet character "A. G. Lambloaf," they hoped that its six eyes and wide smile would appeal to meat-loving children of the seventies.

Sadly, this was not the case.

Make-Ahead Main Dishes /MA**1**

ASPIC-GLAZED LAMB LOAF

Weight Watchers® Recipe Cards

CHICKEN KIEV

Weight Watchers® Recipe Cards

Ah, to be a young ceramic duck in love, and spend many a romantic evening watching the Chicken Kiev get cold. Better than any sunset.

Remember those *Brady Bunch* Hawaii episodes where the Bradys find that tiki idol and bad things start happening to them? This was one of them.

VEAL CHOPS HONOLULU

Weight Watchers® Recipe Cards

STUFFED CABBAGE

Weight Watchers® Recipe Cards

Whoa! That stuffed cabbage is on a cabbage plate. Which totally means it's a big leaf of cabbage stuffed with stuffed cabbage. And dude, what if the stuffed cabbage is *stuffed with more stuffed cabbage?* Which is stuffed with . . . wait. *Dude.* Dude, what if there's another stuffed cabbage . . . THAT WE'RE ALL INSIDE? Like THE WHOLE UNIVERSE? *Whoa.*

Main Dish Malevolence

85

Ever wonder what that movie *Carrie* would have been like if it had been cast with chickens instead of people and also possibly entirely reconceived as a porno?

No? Well, does it help to know that now you'll never have to? No?

Worldwide Favorites /19

ROAST CHICKEN, ITALIAN-STYLE

Weight Watchers® Recipe Cards

VEAL ROLLS SUPREME

Weight Watchers® Recipe Cards

Did you ever have a hankering for veal but just didn't want to deal with the hassle of confining, milk-feeding, and killing your own? Veal Rolls Supreme let you have your veal on the go! Put one in your pocket for a quick veal snack! Why wait sixteen to eighteen weeks of time-consuming calf imprisonment? Have a Veal Roll *now!*

The Amazing Mackerel Pudding Plan

It's a good thing this chicken comes with sporty racing stripes, since you'll want to eat it really fast, just to get it over with.

Classic Adaptations

6

CHICKEN CORDON BLEU

Weight Watchers® Recipe Cards

88

LIVER PÂTÉ EN MASQUE

Weight Watchers® Recipe Cards

I'd thought up a caption for this, but it had the word *bukkake* in it and even *I* have limits.

They developed this recipe at the height of the seventies tanning pill craze, but they decided not to call it *Fake-Baked* Chicken, lest they tip off the FDA to their secret ingredient.

Budget Best Bets /13

LIME-BAKED CHICKEN

Weight Watchers® Recipe Cards

CROWN ROAST OF FRANKFURTERS

Weight Watchers® Recipe Cards

Can you believe there are people out there who buy *actual crown roast* instead of just cooking up a bunch of hot dogs and standing them on end and pinning them together with toothpicks to make a crude barrel to hold a bunch of wet cabbage? Suckers.

Oh, this is lasagna all right, only without tomato sauce. And noodles. And . . . okay, did they run out of quotation marks? Because this is clearly "LASAGNA."

SPINACH LASAGNA

Weight Watchers® Recipe Cards

CHICKEN BAKE

Weight Watchers® Recipe Cards

Chicken bake. Children cry.

All I know about this dish is that it's meat. And that the meat's, uh . . . *Caucasian.*

CAUCASIAN SHASHLIK

Weight Watchers® Recipe Cards

Budget Best Bets | 2

BEST-EVER BARBECUED CHICKEN

Weight Watchers® Recipe Cards

Best-ever use of a prop! Because nothing goes with chicken parts better than, uh, *ceramic* chicken parts.

Inspired by the 1972 film *The Poseidon Adventure,* the best way to eat these eggplant boats filled with tuna is to flip them over. And then panic and scream, "WE'RE ALL GOING TO DIE!"

Convenience Fish /21

TUNA-EGGPLANT POSEIDON

Weight Watchers® Recipe Cards

AFRICADO CHICKEN

Weight Watchers® Recipe Cards

And here is a scene from "Africado Chicken," a Swahili folktale about a friendly blue frog and his chicken friend!

You may have already figured out it doesn't have a happy ending.

as with the haiku
we take Japanese cuisine
and fuck it all up

Classic Adaptations /22

SUKIYAKI

Weight Watchers® Recipe Cards

FRANKFURTER SPECTACULAR

Weight Watchers® Recipe Cards

I would almost be willing to up-holster a whole damn pineapple with pork product just to be able to *say* I was serving Frank-furter Spectacular. Say it with me: Frankfurter! Spectacular!

There's no need to eat it when you can keep your mouth busy for *hours* just by repeating its name.

FRANKFURTER SPECTACULAR!

DRINKS, DESSERTS, DISMAY

Because the *only* thing that was keeping you from downing a seven-ounce jar of pimientos all at once was *having to chew them.*

Snacks, Beverages, and Light Meals / 16

PIMIENTO PURÉE

Weight Watchers® Recipe Cards

Favorite Desserts 5

BREAD PUDDING WITH HARD SAUCE

Weight Watchers® Recipe Cards

Also known as "Bread Pudding with Hard Truth." The *truth* being: Bread pudding looks like cat puke.

These are the saddest diet beverages ever.

The one on the right is skim milk and orange pulp. The one on the left is made with water, sherry extract, and two beef bouillon cubes.

No, really.

Well, there's also celery in it. Oh, and SELF-LOATHING.

Snacks, Beverages, and Light Meals /20

SLENDER QUENCHERS

Weight Watchers® Recipe Cards

LIME SPECIAL

Weight Watchers® Recipe Cards

What makes this Lime Special special? BEEF BROTH.

I wish I were kidding.

The props here tell us that this scene is from the first season of *Little House on the Prairie.* You know—that episode where Pa Ingalls brings home some of them fancy oranges from the city, and nobody knows what the hell to do with them because they're in a little freaking house on the prairie. And Ma tries making a pie with them, but nobody eats the pie except Mary, because she's blind.

Favorite Desserts /20

PUMPKIN-ORANGE MÉLANGE

Weight Watchers® Recipe Cards

COFFEE BUBBLERS

Weight Watchers® Recipe Cards

This is coffee and *diet orange soda,* but that's not what's bubbling, is it?

No, that would be your stomach.

This doesn't look half bad until you consider it's served in the same cups as Fluffy Mackerel Pudding. And nothing can ever be the same after Fluffy Mackerel Pudding. Not even the *idea* of pudding.

PINEAPPLE RICE PUDDING

Weight Watchers® Recipe Cards

MINT FRAPPÈ

Weight Watchers® Recipe Cards

Apparently it's not just a joke: leprechauns really *do* walk into bars.

Where do I even begin here? Which bowl is Siegfried's? Which one is Roy's?

What is going on here? What? What is the meaning of Jell-O, and peaches, and a ceramic cheetah, and paper flowers? And . . . freaky dried-pod thingies? What are those?

Should we smoke them? *Have* we been smoking them?

Worldwide Favorites /16

PEACH MELBA

Weight Watchers® Recipe Cards

ORANGE-GLAZED PUDDING CAKE

Weight Watchers® Recipe Cards

Why not have a little tetanus with your dessert? It perks you up better than coffee! Well, not so much "perks" as "stiffens." Same difference, right?

Drinks, Desserts, Dismay

111

It's a simple recipe, at least until you add the plutonium.

Favorite Desserts

FD**1**

AMBROSIAL LIME SHERBET

Weight Watchers® Recipe Cards

Favorite Desserts /10

CHOCOLATE-PINEAPPLE CAKE

Weight Watchers® Recipe Cards

Here's a simple test. Look at that piece of cake: What kind of sauce is on top?

If your first thought was "hollandaise," you've seen way too many of these recipe cards, and you may need help.

Don't know whether to serve your guests coffee, dessert, or cocktails after dinner? Serve this and leave it open to interpretation! Potential lively discussion questions include: "Is coffee still coffee when it's in Jell-O form?" "Does putting something in a glass make it a drink?" and "Dear God, *what the hell is this?*"

Favorite Desserts / **11**

COFFEE RUM STRATA

Weight Watchers® Recipe Cards

ORANGE "ZABAGLIONE"

Weight Watchers® Recipe Cards

If you didn't know what "zabaglione" was, you'd think, from this photo, that it's an Italian word for "expanding foam sealant," and that you could weatherproof your house with the leftovers.

It was the seventies. Peaches already came in the requisite "goldenrod" color, but it took a little more work to make them modular enough for your space-age kitchen.

Favorite Desserts /17

PEACHY CAKE

Weight Watchers® Recipe Cards

CHOCOLATE "PIE"

Weight Watchers® Recipe Cards

Sometimes quotation marks aren't enough. Not when "pie" means "a crust made of toasted bread crumbs, an egg-and-gelatin filling with green and red food coloring, and meringue made with Sweet'n Low."

Seriously, our current system of punctuation can't even *begin* to convey how NOT AT ALL PIE this "pie" is.

Drinks, Desserts, Dismay

Ah, Grasshopper, you learn fast. Sometimes things are not what they seem. Sometimes, the dragon is not a dragon; only a shadow. And sometimes the drink is not a drink, but a Nerf Ball stuffed in a brandy snifter.

It is not for you to ask why.

Snacks, Beverages, and Light Meals / 8

GRASSHOPPER

Weight Watchers® Recipe Cards

Snacks, Beverages, and Light Meals / 3

"COCKTAIL FAVORITES"

Weight Watchers® Recipe Cards

One of these "cocktail favorites" is made with diet black-cherry soda, the other with instant chicken broth.

Just a hunch, but I don't think they're going to get me "drunk."

Drinks, Desserts, Dismay

119

With the rise of popular psychology in the seventies, this combination dessert and Rorschach test proved to be a big hit, and an ideal diet dish, too.

Because once you've seen a headless armadillo playing jai alai in your dessert as a result of projected unresolved anger from unspecified childhood issues—well, you don't feel so hungry anymore.

Favorite Desserts /13

FROZEN FRUIT PURÉE

Weight Watchers® Recipe Cards

Favorite Desserts

8

CHOCOLATE "BROWNIE" DESSERT

Weight Watchers® Recipe Cards

You know, these "brownies" actually *look* like brownies, so I have to wonder about the quotation marks. "Brownies," huh? Why must you be so wink-winky, O Seventies Brownie Recipe? What's *your* secret?

Oh. Oh *yeah.*